Antisocial Personality Disorder: The Ultimate Guide to Symptoms, Treatment and Prevention

By: Clayton Geoffreys

Table of Contents

Disclaimer

This book is not intended as a substitute for the medical advice of a psychologist, physician, or medical professional. The reader should regularly visit a doctor or therapist in matters relating to his or her health and particularly with respect to symptoms that may require medical diagnosis or attention.

Foreword

Personality disorders can significantly alter the way one lives their life. Understanding the symptoms of these disorders is important for everyone. Whether or not you personally suffer from these disorders, learning to recognize symptoms is the first step to being able to best assist someone who may be suffering from a condition. Psychologists have studied disorders for many years, creating multiple iterations of diagnosis tools; it's difficult to truly pinpoint everything with 100% accuracy, but with time and further research, we as a society will become better aware of the nature of these disorders. Hopefully from reading *Antisocial Personality Disorder: The Ultimate Guide to Symptoms, Treatment and Prevention,* I can pass along some of the abundance of information I have learned about Antisocial Personality Disorder (ASPD), including its symptoms, therapies to consider, and ways to begin overcoming ASPD. Thank you for downloading my book. Hope you enjoy and if you do, please do not forget to leave a review! Also, check out my website at claytongeoffreys.com to join my exclusive list where I let you know about my latest books. To thank you for your purchase, you can go to my site to download a free copy of _33 Life Lessons: Success Principles, Career Advice & Habits of Successful People_. In the book, you'll learn from some of the greatest thought leaders of different industries on what it takes to become successful and how to live a great life.

Cheers,

Clayton Geoffreys

What is Antisocial Personality Disorder?

Antisocial Personality Disorder (ASPD) is a character dysfunction that prevents an individual from engaging with society in a normal manner. Individuals with Antisocial Personality Disorder are typically unable to become reliable members of society as their disorder hinders their ability to meaningfully participate in family, business, or educational opportunities. The reason for this hindrance is due to their nature generally classified as displaying excessive levels of self-importance, blatant disregard for others' rights, and a marked tendency to exhibit callous, cynical attitudes towards others. These individuals are also more likely to engage in amoral behavior that is unacceptable by societal standards.

To understand a disorder such as Antisocial Personality Disorder, one must truly understand the individual diagnosed. This presents a problem in terms of general study, as it is impossible to fully grasp and understand another person whom you have never met before. However, there are, in general, some characteristics and commonalities that allow for a base understanding of those with Antisocial Personality Disorder, which gives a researcher insight into how this disorder develops.

Those who are diagnosed with Antisocial Personality Disorder tend to share a very narcissistic view of themselves. These individuals are not modest individuals, but rather, believe themselves to be above others in essentially every category for which they place value. If they can or do acknowledge their lack in any area, such as academics, looks, or musical talent, for example, they will have a correspondingly low evaluation of that area. Areas in which they excel, they will place an emphasis on in terms of overall importance when regarding a person's 'value'. This safeguards their high opinion of themselves, which is a critical aspect of their personality. Ironically, this narcissistic attitude often covers a lack of self-confidence, and these individuals may have underlying self-esteem issues that need to be addressed.

In addition to their highly narcissistic views, these individuals are often highly manipulative. While they do not see a great deal of intrinsic value in others, they do see the more tangible benefits that others can provide, and they will not hesitate to take advantage of others in order to ensure their own comfort or advancement. With this motivation, some of those with antisocial personalities can, upon occasion, display considerable skill in manipulating others for their own purposes. This manipulation may include some degree of charm, which in turn may cause others to doubt the original diagnosis of Antisocial Personality Disorder. However, this charm is nothing more than a surface layer they produced through cold calculability to ensure their own standing and does not speak of the underlying motives or thoughts of the individual. When the target of their charm has lost their usability, they will display the same blatant disregard for that person and their emotions as they do toward others.

This attitude is a natural barrier against forming close, meaningful relationships with others. Therefore, in addition to their inability to interact with others in a normal fashion, people with Antisocial Personality Disorder are also frequently isolated in the social stratum. This isolation hampers and, in large measure, prevents them from developing normal, healthy friendships. This lack of friendship during critical years serves as a double-edged sword. While those with Antisocial Personality Disorder already struggle to grasp the concept of "empathy", they are simultaneously isolated from their peers. This often reinforces their negative views toward others.

These views usually become prominent during the teenage or young adult years. Because this is a critical period of time for personality development, those who are beginning to develop antisocial behavior during this period may suffer severe repercussions in terms of social standing and future opportunities. For example, teenagers who are starting to develop Antisocial Personality Disorder may alienate their peers, resulting in their own social isolation. This isolation may serve as a contributing factor to negative behavior, such as skipping class or even taking part in more serious dangerous activities, such as drinking alcohol or taking drugs. These behaviors will have an obvious negative impact on their ability to maintain grades or make beneficial life choices, such as preparing for college. It is, therefore, common for those with antisocial personalities to become high-school dropouts with the corresponding increased risk for negative future life experiences.

For individuals of this nature, maturity, as recognized by the general population, will be something they struggle with. Rather than behaving as calm, rational adults, these individuals typically experience a 'stall-out' in their emotional growth, which impairs their ability to make responsible decisions. While accepting responsibility for your own behavior and acknowledging personal mistakes are essential characteristics of adulthood and maturity, those with Antisocial Personality Disorder are incapable of doing so. This lack of maturity leads to increased impulsivity, a lack of forethought in decision making, and high levels of selfishness.

Moreover, these negative attributes affect more than the individuals' attitude toward educational or career opportunities. In the personal realm, those with Antisocial Personality Disorder suffer a range of serious setbacks. While every relationship they have is affected by their disorder, their relationships with a romantic or sexual nature are more overtly affected. Individuals with Antisocial Personality Disorder are often highly manipulative in these relationships. They may become very exploitive of their partners, while their own behaviors are likely to be consistently irresponsible. These individuals are often sexually promiscuous and may begin displaying sexual behavior at a relatively young age. In line with this, individuals with Antisocial Personality Disorder often commit infidelity against their mates, which can lead to divorce. These individuals are also known to consistently and frequently lie to their partner and engage in unsafe sexual practices. Having sexual relationships with strangers, engaging in illicit affairs, and other equally troubling behaviors of similar nature are traits often observed from people with ASPD.

While the impact of their Antisocial Personality Disorder is most easily seen in their romantic relationships, they are not the only relationships affected. Relationships with parents, children, and siblings are, likewise affected in an extremely negative way and can cause considerable levels of stress on the overall family structure. The inherently selfish nature of those with Antisocial Personality Disorder, coupled with a high level of immaturity and impulsivity make successful, responsible parenting a difficult task. Caring for a child requires a level of sensitivity, forethought and selflessness that those with Antisocial Personality Disorder do not have. In addition, a child is likely to be seen as a burden by those with Antisocial Personality Disorder unless, or until, that child can provide them with some form of reward for their efforts.

Likewise, those with Antisocial Personality Disorder are most likely to be manipulative of their parents and may cause considerable strain on their relationship with them. As previously mentioned, those with Antisocial Personality Disorder are often highly immature and they may rely heavily on their parents' support even through their adult years. Their relationships with their siblings are also likely to be negatively affected by resentment and jealously that they feel. This negative relationship is likely to be reinforced by the siblings who will frequently resent the person with ASPD for causing such stress on their family unit, and the person with ASPD will resent his or her siblings. It is, therefore, no surprise that family relationships, which include a member with Antisocial Personality Disorder, are often extremely dysfunctional. It is important to note, however, that while the family of those with Antisocial Personality Disorder is often dysfunctional, the family unit can also play a critical role in the treatment and successful management of the patient's disorder. People with ASPD are unlikely to have friends outside the family. Therefore, the only source of support they often receive is through their family.

11

This may appear to be a harsh critique of those with Antisocial Personality Disorder but what is important to remember here is that, as with every disorder, individuals will fall into a continuum of these characteristics. Those who are more severely affected by this disorder are likely to be more manipulative, selfish, and narcissistic than their less-affected counterparts. Likewise, not every patient will display the same set of behaviors as others. Some individuals may even become more capable parents (though being termed 'natural' is unlikely) than others. Due to these variations, Theodore Milton has identified five subtypes of Antisocial Personality Disorder. These subtypes are known as Malevolent Antisocial, Covetous Antisocial, Risk-Taking Antisocial, Reputation-Defending Antisocial, and Nomadic Antisocial.

The 5 Subtypes of Antisocial Personality Disorder

Theodore Millon is a noted American psychologist who was most known for his work on personality disorder subtypes. He is credited with identifying subtypes for multiple personality disorders, including Schizoid Personality Disorder, Obsessive-Compulsive Personality Disorder, Narcissistic Personality Disorder, and of course, Antisocial Personality Disorder. There are five subtypes that Millon identified for Antisocial Personality Disorder. Each subtype has its own characteristics and challenges for the patient, and patients should consider their own subtype when seeking treatment or diagnosis.

Malevolent Antisocial Personality Subtype

Those who fall into the malevolent subtype of Antisocial Personality Disorder can be thought of as your 'classic villain'. This is not to say that those individuals linked to this subtype are 'evil' but, rather, people belonging to the malevolent subtype tend to display features and characteristics that reflects the historic portrayal of villainous characters. These individuals are typically brutal, vicious people. This may be the direct result of the individual's inability to experience empathy from those around them. But whatever the cause, they are often extraordinarily harsh towards others. This brutality is not only displayed through verbal or social mediums, but may also reflect in direct physical attacks committed by the patient.

This is especially true if the patient feels that they have been wronged in any way. When they sense that their values and ideas are under attack, they will respond with vicious force. Revenge is an idea that holds great appeal for those in the malevolent subtype and they hold no compunction about carrying out acts to achieve this aim. Moreover, those in the malevolent subtype are unlikely to be restricted in their aims by an overly developed conscience.

While not recognized as a diagnosable disorder by wider psychological circles, in more criminal justice oriented settings, these individuals are frequently classified as either sociopaths or psychopaths. There is a slight distinction between the two, which renders some conflict in professional circles over the classification of these individuals. However, it is sufficient to say that these individuals suffer from a severe abnormality in the area of conscience, to the extent that the individual may be perceived to lack a conscience at all. This impairment of the conscience enables the malevolent subtype individual to take actions that others might find untenable. Paired with the general want for revenge displayed by these individuals, those in this subtype can take drastic, malicious actions against others that can result in serious injury.

Moreover, the malevolent antisocial individual anticipates betrayal from others. This expectation leads the patient to assume a defensive position prior to an attack, resulting in the patient taking preemptive action. In real world terms, those in this subtype often attack others before they themselves are attacked in an effort to guard themselves. Furthermore, rather than feel some semblance of remorse or regret for their actions, individuals in this subtype are likely to display a callous, belligerent attitude in regards to their own behavior. To this patient, the most important person is, in fact, himself or herself. Therefore, any action taken to protect themselves, or to punish those who have harmed them in any fashion, is perfectly acceptable behavior. Instead of believing themselves to be in the wrong, they firmly believe that their own actions are both justifiable and reasonable.

Covetous Antisocial Personality Disorder Subtype

It may come as no surprise that one of the defining characteristics of the covetous subtype of Antisocial Personality Disorder is a marked penchant for greed. It may be said that all individuals are greedy in some aspect, and this is likely true. However, for those individuals who fall into the covetous subtype, their greed extends beyond normal bounds and affects both how they view the world and their relationships with others. The wants and desires of these individuals become an integral part of their personality and they are driven to gain these things regardless of cost or prior ownership.

In fact, the covetous antisocial will only want something more if it is denied them, or if ownership has already been established by another. For these individuals, a large part of their pleasure in realizing their wants and desires is not so much as having, but in

17

taking. This presents several problems for the patient with regards to a social setting. In some instances, this desire may lead to serious and potentially illegal actions that can have serious repercussions. In addition, it is obvious that this tendency to want what others have will lead to some measure of friction with those who claim prior ownership. Therefore this tendency may lead not only to trouble with legal authorities, but also with peers, associates, and others.

Moreover, these individuals feel intentionally denied by others. For these individuals, taking what others have is a measure they deem both necessary and appropriate. This is largely because they do not believe that others will freely give what they believe they deserve. Moreover, these individuals tend to believe that they deserve quite a lot. Paired with their often irresponsible, selfish, and frankly slothful behavior, earning what they believe they deserve is a difficult task for these individuals. The disparity between what they perceive they deserve and what they are capable of earning for themselves is simply too great in many instances. This can lead to resentment towards others of behalf of the patient, while also reaffirming their 'If I want it, I'll take it' attitude.

Their naturally envious nature leads these individuals to yet another difficulty in their disorder. Not only are they envious of others, these individuals frequently are seeking retribution against others. The reason why these individuals desire retribution may vary widely from imagined slights to open jealousy. If these individuals believe that another was inappropriately rewarded in their stead, for example, they are likely to wish for retribution on both the one who gave the award and the recipient.

Risk-Taking Antisocial Personality Disorder Subtype

The risk-taking subtype of Antisocial Personality Disorder is highly interesting. Persons under the risk-taking subtype are not characterized by intrinsic traits, such as greed or cruelty, but are rather noted for their brash behavior. Perhaps due to the lack of overall maturity developed, those in this subtype are known for their reckless actions, most notably those actions that pose significant risks to their safety and others'. This may also be due to the patient's lack of impulse control, a widely accepted trait of those with antisocial personality disorder.

This lack of impulse control may vary depending on the individual. For those of the covetous subtype, for example, this lack of impulse control may take the form of theft. Those in the malevolent subtype, however, may manifest this trait by striking others in anger. However, for the risk-taking subtype, this lack of control reveals itself in dangerous and impetuous actions, such as driving under the influence, speeding, and extreme sports.

This subtype is dominated by an audacious character type that plays well in movies but in real-life constitutes serious risk. Though they are best known for their reckless behavior, these individuals still have the narcissistic tendencies that Antisocial Personality Disorder is associated with. These tendencies, combined with their bold character, can certainly alienate others. This subtype is, however, probably the least likely to truly estrange themselves from others. While the negative traits of Antisocial Personality Disorder are still present, their focus on high-risk behaviors and occasional displays of charm can create a certain appeal to others.

This subtype of Antisocial Personality Disorder includes histrionic features, meaning they regularly display attention-seeking behaviors and extreme emotionality. Consistent with the other subtypes of Antisocial Personality Disorder, the risk-taking individual does feel a sense of superiority over others.

However, these individuals need to be the focus of those around them, and are often ardent in their pursuit of attention. These are the standout individuals – think famous, popular people who simultaneously need the adoration of others while believing those same individuals are inferior to them.

It may seem that this is a preferable form for antisocial behavior to take, and in some regard one might be correct. However, there are negative aspects to this subtype that should not be overlooked. For instance, while their risky antics and dramatic style might engender some form of awe from others, these individuals are unlikely to have true, meaningful relationships. They are not immune from the negative aspects of Antisocial Personality Disorder, which makes them often have difficulty establishing and maintaining relationships. They are highly narcissistic and easily insulted, and the negative opinions of those around them may seriously affect their happiness. It is therefore important to remember that, while the negative facets of other subtypes may be more immediately noticeable, the risk-taking subtype also has negative attributes.

Reputation-Defending Antisocial Personality Disorder Subtype

The reputation-defending subtype of Antisocial Personality Disorder is most appropriately named. To individuals of this subtype, their reputation acts as a form of armor. For them, their reputation is something that establishes their superiority over others, while at the same time prevents them from being harmed by others. These individuals need others to see them as a perfect person, as someone who has no flaws to exploit or weakness to take advantage of.

By necessity, the individual format of this reputation will vary due to the circumstances of the individual involved. For example, a 1950s era woman with this subtype might need others to see her as the perfect housewife. She would want no rumors about her family, hide anything that didn't fit her 'perfect' image, and use this reputation to ruthlessly judge her contemporaries. This reputation would take a vastly different form for a modern woman, who might want to be seen as the perfect businesswoman. Her reputation may be based on her ruthlessness and logic, her cold practicality, or her cutting intelligence. She would need to protect her reputation against rumors of her softness, that being a woman has impacted her ability to lead, or that she has allowed her emotions control her actions.

The point of these examples is not to point out the stereotypes of different eras but to rather emphasize that the time and place in which people under the reputation-defending subtype find themselves plays a large role in the type of reputation they wish to establish. What will not change based on these outside factors is that they need to be seen as 'perfect' by their contemporaries. Moreover, in addition to being seen as 'perfect' by others, these individuals need to be seen as 'unbreakable' or 'untouchable' in the eyes of others. Though this is of course a façade, people of this subtype use that façade to protect them and to discourage attacks from outside parties against them. Due to this, they place a high degree of importance on appearance and become steadfast when their position is threatened.

In the same manner, those of this subtype are tenacious when protecting their reputation. They are likely to take serious action when they feel that their reputation is being threatened by others and will have no problem resorting to drastic measures to ensure their own success. For these patients, their reputation is a valuable core aspect of their identification. While their actions may seem exaggerated to others, the reputation-defending subtype are simply protecting a critical aspect of themselves. Likewise, these individuals respond to threats to their reputation much like how others might respond when their honor or ethics are questioned or threatened.

Nomadic Antisocial Personality Disorder Subtype

The nomadic antisocial individual is a person who is often found on the peripheral of society. One could even call them the 'forgotten' in modern society. They are characterized by gypsy-like traits, such that they rarely establish a place for themselves among society. Rather, they wander throughout their life, never truly finding a place that suits them enough to stay. This drifting goes beyond their physical location – they drift from job to job, relationship to relationship, never truly cementing themselves to anyone or anything.

They are the dropouts and misfits, who feel as though they are society leftovers. Often this can lead these individuals to become vagrants, and they may frequently experience both poverty and homelessness.

26

Though others may place the blame for this solely on the individuals' actions, the patient will often feel as if they are 'jinxed'. These individuals often have higher levels of self-pity. They may not find value in exerting much effort as they believe that no matter the effort they put in they will not receive a positive outcome.

The nomadic subtype has features of both the avoidant and schizoid personalities. This is a heavy combination that, once paired with the natural features of Antisocial Personality Disorder, naturally produces negative results. The avoidant features that present themselves in the nomadic subtype may be responsible for the tendency of the patient to move on rather than struggle to establish themselves in a given position. This itinerant behavior has two major drawbacks for the patient. First, they are unable to create any real bond with others. This lack of bond with others limits the patient's resources, in both their physical and emotional capacity. Whereas others are able to rely on

27

friends and family in times of need, their avoidant nature ensures that the nomadic antisocial is isolated. Secondly, their escapist tendencies prevent the patient from taking action to address their underlying problems, including their negative attitude.

Their schizoid feature reinforces the difficulties these individuals face in establishing bonds or facing their own shortcomings. A schizoid trait refers to an individual's difficulty in establishing relationships with others, particularly due to their inability to either express or respond to emotions. This lack of emotion and apparent detachment results to schizoid features regularly taking the role of the 'loner' who is without friends and appears not to need any. However, as it has already been established, a relationship with others is critical for both financial and mental health. The lack of these bonds promotes the conditions for those of the nomadic subtype to become isolated from society and experience all the difficulties that come with that isolation.

What Causes Antisocial Personality Disorder?

Antisocial Personality Disorder, like most personality disorders, is believed to be the result of a combination of factors. These factors come in two different regards: genetic or biological factors, which include risk factors, such as hereditary factors, chemical or hormonal imbalances, or early brain damage and environmental factors, which include home life, socialization, learning, etc. The more these risk factors are present for a given individual, the greater the chance that he or she will develop Antisocial Personality Disorder. However, this does not mean that all individuals who have some or even all of these risk factors present in them will, in fact, develop Antisocial Personality Disorder. Diagnosis should be carried out by a professional and must be based on behavior, not risk factors.

Biological Factors

Humans are complex beings. There are so many minute details that are critical to the stability of an individual that isolating a single factor in irregular development is a difficult, if not impossible, task. For this reason, there are many different theories on which biological factors increase an individual's chance for developing Antisocial Personality Disorder. Moreover, several different theories have some evidence of their veracity. Therefore, it is highly likely that more than one of these theories are correct and that the greater the combination of these factors, the more likely an individual is to develop Antisocial Personality Disorder.

One of the biological theories for Antisocial Personality Disorder is that it is a result of an abnormal development of the nervous system. The nervous system is a network of cells and fibers that transmit nerve impulses (thoughts and actions) from one part of the body to another. Ultimately, the nervous system controls our thoughts and actions. If an individual has an abnormality in their nervous system, this abnormality can cause serious issues for that person. Identifying an abnormality in the nervous system can be a difficult task. Learning disorders, consistent long-term bedwetting, and hyperactivity are all possible indications of an abnormality in the nervous system. If an individual displays these attributes, there might be an increased risk for that person to also model antisocial behavior.

Another biological risk factor for Antisocial Personality Disorder is maternal smoking during pregnancy. Scientists believe that when a mother smokes during pregnancy, the oxygen provided to the fetus is impaired. This lack of oxygen may result in minor forms of brain injury to the unborn child. While this damage may not be immediately observable or affect the physical health of the child (though other effects of prenatal smoking certainly do), later in development, this damage might eventually have a significant impact. Studies showed that those individuals whose mother smoked while pregnant are more likely to exhibit antisocial behavior, engage in delinquent behavior, and have issues with conduct.

Sensory input is also linked to Antisocial Personality Disorder. There is evidence that those who require a greater amount of sensory input are prone to Antisocial Personality Disorder. Sensory input refers to a person's ability to organize and use the information relayed to them through their senses. In individuals with a low natural sensory input, there is a chance that they may take part in more risky activities to raise their arousal levels, thereby satisfying their need for increased sensory input. The evidence that antisocial patients have low resting heart rates as well as low skin conductance supports this theory. Brain scans have also shown that those who have antisocial personality disorder have lower levels on certain brain measures, reinforcing the idea that sensory input may affect the antisocial behavior of the patient.

Aside from this sensory input, abnormal brain function has also been linked to antisocial behavior. This theory is based on the knowledge that the temporal lobes and prefrontal cortex control both mood and behavior. If these areas of the brain are functioning improperly, or have been damaged to some degree, antisocial behavior may result. Likewise, serotonin is also believed to be a potential cause of Antisocial Personality Disorder. Serotonin is a neurotransmitter, which helps relay signals in the brain. If the levels of serotonin are imbalanced, mood and thought processes can be affected. For this reason, serotonin imbalances have been linked to depression, as well as Antisocial Personality Disorder.

There is also the chance that Antisocial Personality Disorder can be inherited through a direct hereditary link. This is evidenced by the large recognition that those who are diagnosed with Antisocial Personality Disorder are frequently the children of antisocial individuals themselves. This is a link that can usually be followed throughout generations, as well as across familial trees, to establish a pattern of a direct hereditary cause.

Environment Factors

Just as genetic or biological factors play a large role in determining the chances of developing Antisocial Personality Disorder; environmental factors can also be contributing factors. The social environment begins with the parents, so it is no surprise that children with antisocial parents are more likely to be antisocial themselves. Antisocial parents are unlikely to be able to provide a stable home environment, or provide the necessary emotional support for a child to develop normally. In the absence of this stability, and paired with the limited emotional feedback they receive, children may learn to display antisocial behavior themselves. Though, of course, some may argue that this is a point for a hereditary link to antisocial behavior as well.

A link has been established between the conduct of parents and the behavior of their children. For example, a large study found a correlation between the status of delinquent boys and alcoholic parents. Parents of delinquent boys have been found to be more likely to have criminal pasts and tendencies, and there is often a presence of divorce or separation. The absence of a parent is a particularly high risk factor for children to develop Antisocial Personality Disorder. The theory to explain this link is that the lack of a parental bond prevents the child from feeling secure in a social situation. Isolated from this crucial bond, the child learns to isolate him or herself from others as well.

This is also believed as the reason for the increased risk for antisocial behavior among adopted children. Children for adoption are frequently moved from home to home prior to being permanently placed with a family. This movement from home to home often happens during a critical period in a child's development, which can have severe repercussions on the child's psyche. The inability to form a long-term bond during this period, along with a sense of isolation and abandonment, can cause the child to become withdrawn from all those around them. The ultimate result of such a situation is the development of antisocial behavior, potentially leading to Antisocial Personality Disorder later on. While the diagnosis of Antisocial Personality Disorder can only be made after a person reaches 18 years old, children who are seen to be at risk for the development of this disorder and given preemptive care may reduce, or even eliminate, the negative effects of this disorder.

Overall, the development of Antisocial Personality Disorder is likely due to a convergence of multiple risk factors. Being genetically predisposed or biologically prone to this personality disorder certainly plays a large part in whether a person develops an antisocial personality. However, it is rare for these factors alone to produce Antisocial Personality Disorder. Oftentimes, there is a genetic predisposition that is triggered by an environmental factor, which results to the disorder. However, the psychological community has established no formal cause of Antisocial Personality Disorder. This is, in part, due to the difficulty of distinguishing what kinds of risk factors for Antisocial Personality Disorder are causation factors and which factors are correlation factors. Causation factors are factors that have a direct impact on the development of a disorder or condition. Correlation factors refer to elements that may be present simultaneously with a disorder but are independent of the disorder. In the case of Antisocial Personality Disorder, determining what is a cause and what is a correlation factor to the disorder is complicated by the limited viable research methods, the late term diagnosis, and the intricacy of the factors themselves.

The 9 Most Common Symptoms of Antisocial Personality Disorder

1. Disregard for Right or Wrong

Patients with Antisocial Personality Disorder often disregard society's concept of 'right' or 'wrong' behavior. This is the result of two aspects of the antisocial personality- the lack of a social bond, and a narcissistic outlook. Those with Antisocial Personality Disorder often fail to establish strong bonds with the rest of society, and so, they are not bound by the social mores society uses to maintain peace and harmony. For example, even if there are no formal rules in a group, unspoken rules will exist. These rules serve to keep the group homogenous and reinforce the strong bond between the individuals that compose the group. Breaking those rules may result in isolation or alienation from those individuals, which serves as a motivator to follow established rules. Those with

Antisocial Personality Disorder lack these bonds and, thus are not hampered by a need to be liked or accepted by others, releasing them from the need to behave 'correctly'. This freedom is compounded by the narcissistic viewpoint of these individuals. Not only are they free from emotional motivation to do the 'right' thing, they also believe themselves to be above others. This creates a situation in which these patients feel they are above the rules. This trait also encourages the patient to place their own wants and concerns above those of others, thereby leading the patient to make the best decision for their interests, rather than the morally or socially acceptable choice.

2. Manipulating Others

Patients with Antisocial Personality Disorder are known for their ability and willingness to manipulate others. The reason for this manipulation may vary by person or by circumstance, and can be for either personal gain or simply because they enjoy doing so.

In general, these individuals believe that they are above others. Therefore, they have little compunction about manipulating other 'lesser' people for their own satisfaction. Some of these individuals may even justify their manipulation internally, excusing their behavior because 'it won't hurt anyone' or 'it doesn't matter'. Others may be so isolated from the social norm that they do not feel the need for this justification. They believe that they are only doing what they want and the responsibility lies with the party who is allowing themselves to be manipulated.

This form of manipulation may vary as well. Oftentimes, the form of manipulation the patient chooses will be selected based on what they believe has the best chance of success. In some instances, this may require lying. Those with Antisocial Personality Disorder are known to be frequent liars to some degree. If the patient believes that lying to someone will garner the reaction they want, they are unlikely to hesitate to do so. However, in cases in which lying is not a possibility, these individuals can and will resort to using their charm to manipulate others. These individuals are quite cunning and they are often able to win over others, presenting themselves entirely as another type of individual. This image is used to manipulate the other party until such a time when the patient no longer needs them. At that point, they will often cease their charade of charm or stop contact entirely with the other person.

3. Extreme Egocentrism

Those who are egocentric are worried first and foremost with their own concerns. They are 'me' people, focused on their own wants, needs, and desires. For the patient with Antisocial Personality Disorder, this preoccupation with the self is even more prominent. The number one priority they have is their own self-advancement. To achieve their goals, they will resort to any means, such as lying, cheating, stealing… none of it matters, so long as they benefit from their actions. While it may seem counterintuitive, this extreme focus on their own desires acts as a stumbling block to their own personal development, their relationships with others, and ultimately, their own success in life. Individuals cannot succeed without the help of others, and constantly placing your own wants and needs above those of others is unlikely to inspire them to offer help when the time comes.

Altruistic behavior, or self-sacrificing for the benefit of others, is something people with Antisocial Personality Disorder cannot understand. The best way to comprehend this trait of the antisocial individual is to understand that to the patient with Antisocial Personality Disorder, life is a war and every interaction they have with others is perceived to be a battle. In this 'war' the only person the antisocial person is fighting for is himself or herself. Seen in this manner, it is easier to grasp the mentality of the Antisocial Personality Disorder patient.

4. Recurring Issues with the Law

The patient with Antisocial Personality Disorder has a range of traits which make him or her more likely to come into contact with law enforcement in a negative way. To begin with, individuals with Antisocial Personality Disorder have a problem with authority figures of any kind. This begins with their parents, remains true with teachers, and eventually leads to law enforcement. These individuals simply do not have a great deal of tolerance or respect for the rules of others, even when the 'others' are police or society in general. They are therefore more likely to break the law, especially in more petty ways such as shoplifting or speeding.

While such petty crimes might be more prevalent among people with ASPD, they are certainly at risk to engage in more serious crime as well, particularly child abuse or neglect, and more aggressive crimes, such as assault or battery. These actions can lead these individuals to the attention of the police. As such, they frequently have long rap sheets of criminal activity. It is interesting to note that these individuals are also more likely to resist arrest. This is likely the result of the convergence of their naturally aggressive behavior paired with their lack of respect for authority figures. Unfortunately, this can often compound their difficulties with law enforcement and may result in a more serious charge and sentence.

5. Repeated Violations of Others Rights

The rights of others are not of much concern to those with Antisocial Personality Disorder. In all honesty, these patients have a blatant disregard for the rights of others and have absolutely no compunction about violating those rights. 'Rights' refer to the fundamental freedom of a human being that is recognized by society. These rights can include everything from the most basic freedoms, such as making an informed decision, to life-changing elements such as the right of reproduction. This is quite a difficult topic and may prove challenging to grasp at first. To gain a better understanding, it is best to see these violations in context.

For instance, the right to control your ability to have a child, and the right to decide whether or not you wish to have a child, is a fundamental human right. However, if a person with Antisocial Personality Disorder had a different opinion about whether to or not to have a child, they would not hesitate to make that decision solely by themselves, without regard to their partner's rights on the subject. For example, if a female patient with Antisocial Personality Disorder believed that having a child might improve (or save, depending on the state of the relationship) her relationship she might lie to her partner and make a deliberate attempt to get pregnant. In this case, she disregards the right of her partner to decide whether he would like to have a child. Likewise, the reverse could also be true. If a male patient believes that having a child would cement his relationship with a woman, he might also lie or manipulate circumstances to impregnate his companion. This may be an extreme example, but the general essence is the same. These individuals regard their own wants and rights as the only important element in making a decision, and they will repeatedly violate the rights of others in an effort to achieve their own goals.

6. Child Abuse or Neglect

It is difficult for many to understand how someone with Antisocial Personality Disorder parents their child, or more accurately, fails to do so. The first thing one must understand about antisocial parents is the way they view their child. In many cases, those with Antisocial Personality Disorder become parents out of

48

logic or as an accident. These people are, for lack of a better term, very cold individuals. They will not hesitate to produce a child for their selfish reasons. However, when the reason for the child disappears – or once the child has fulfilled its purpose – the antisocial parent often sees the child as a burden rather than a gift. The patient may become pregnant (or impregnate another) by accident, and terminating or adopting the child may not be an option. In this instance, the parent might feel that the child is a burden that drains resources from their most important person – themselves.

Children require great effort, patience, and love from their parents. However, patients with Antisocial Personality Disorder do not have these things to give. Thus, both child abuse and child neglect frequently occur when the parent in question has Antisocial Personality Disorder. Children of these individuals may be physically or mentally abused, becoming the target of their parent's frustrations. They may also be neglected as the primary concern as those with ASPD only consider themselves primary concern number one. Everyone else, even his or her own child, will come second. This can result in malnourishment, lack of health, uncleanliness, and more. Forming a bond with the parent with ASPD is, undeniably, hard to develop and this, in turn, can propagate the cycle, as the child of the patient is also likely to develop Antisocial Personality Disorder.

7. Extreme Negative Emotions

Everyone has a bad day sometimes, and everyone experiences periods of negative emotions. People can be irritable and they can do things impulsively, which they might regret later. These are normal occurrences and do not generally present overly dramatic difficulties in a typical individual's life. However, those with Antisocial Personality Disorder are by no means 'typical'. These individuals will often experience extreme levels of negative, harmful emotions that pose a direct threat to their own and others' mental stability. These negative emotions include hostility, impulsiveness and agitation, and can naturally result in extreme situations. Individuals who experience these emotions in their full intensity are likely to make huge mistakes and terrible decisions, which result to severe repercussions. For instance, they may create conflict with others or engage in self-harm as a result of these negative emotions.

Violence, aggression and irritability are also frequent symptoms of Antisocial Personality Disorder. These harmful emotions can have serious consequences, such as physical violence. Combined with their impulsive nature and natural immaturity, their aggressive behavior can lead them to serious trouble. These emotions are often the underlying reason for their frequent encounters with law enforcement, which might negatively affect personal and business relationships. Overall, these emotions present a serious issue for the patient with Antisocial Personality Disorder. Unless they master their emotions, it may become a detrimental element in the patient's life.

8. Lack of Empathy

Empathy is the ability of an individual to understand another person, enabling an individual to look at a situation with another person's perspective in mind. In an integrated society, empathy is a critical skill, as it allows people to become more forgiving, understanding, and accepting of others. Unfortunately, empathy is an emotional tool that those with Antisocial Personality Disorder almost universally lack. This causes several issues for the patient along with the other issues caused by the disorder. For instance, this lack of empathy curtails the ability of the patient to feel remorse for their actions. Empathy cannot be present without understanding; and if you do not sympathize with another person, there is nothing to stop you from causing harm.

This lack of empathy when combined with being egocentric and narcissistic tendencies, create a completely self-centered individual, believing that they are superior to everyone and unable to empathize with others. They are the perfect specimen to become tyrannical dictators or even serial killers. This is not to say that all individuals who have Antisocial Personality Disorder are serial killers, or are 'evil'. This is absolutely, unequivocally, not the case. However, it cannot be denied that there is certain preponderance in these infamous populations for Antisocial Personality Disorder to be prevalent.

9. Dangerous Behavior

Maturity, practicality, and rationality are the skills helping a person to make reasonable decisions. More importantly, they help prevent a person from making

bad decisions. When these elements are lacking –
imprudent decisions can be made. These irresponsible
decisions often come in the form of dangerous
behavior such as car surfing, drunk driving, texting
while driving, etc. But these behaviors can also include
less obvious forms of dangerous behavior, such as
having unprotected sex with a stranger, engaging in
illegal activities, or taking drugs.

Five Common Therapy Methods for Antisocial Personality Disorder

Treatment for Antisocial Personality Disorder is a difficult, tricky, and long-term affair. Treatment is the most effective when started early or when it starts to manifest, preferably in early childhood or adolescence. Treatment at an early stage is much more likely to have a positive outcome. However, this disorder is not being diagnosed until the patient reaches 18 years of age, early treatment options might not be an option. This presents a problem because older patients with Antisocial Personality Disorder are highly unlikely to seek treatment on their own, and typically do not believe that treatment is necessary at all. Though their disorder can interfere with their lives and overall happiness, patients are unlikely to recognize that fact and rarely find fault with their own behavior. Considering this fact, it can often take a considerable amount of effort before individuals with this condition will seek treatment. Often, patients are required to seek treatment as part of a court-mandated order or as part of their sentencing.

Treatment itself is not an easy or fast process, regardless of what individual chooses as a treatment option. Treatment must generally be conducted on a long-term basis and improvement in condition is linked to the patient's open-mindedness and willingness to improve. If a patient who has been coerced into seeking treatment (and they often must be) is reluctant to change or refuses to admit they have a problem, the treatment process can be ineffective or drawn-out. With that said, there are several options for those who are willing to seek treatment.

1. Psychotherapy

The first of these options is psychotherapy, also known as 'talk-therapy' and known to be the traditional form of treatment. It involves establishing a relationship between a licensed psychologist or psychiatrist and the patient, and using that relationship to help talk the patient through his or her disorder. Over time, the patient can recognize and circumvent the negative aspects of their conditions and learn acceptable coping behaviors. Psychoanalytical treatment options will not typically be successful with this condition. Practitioners should therefore focus on establishing motivation and building connections between good behaviors and positive reinforcements. The key when treating Antisocial Personality Disorder is convincing the patients that they want and need to change the patterns of their behavior. If this is done, some form of success may be achieved. This treatment can be done through individual, group or family sessions. Even friends can participate in the therapy session, so long as a skilled practitioner is conducting the session.

There are no harmful side effects to this treatment option.

However, the disadvantage to the psychotherapy treatment option is that results are not guaranteed. If patients refuse to see that they have a problem and are unwilling to address the issue, the results gained from psychotherapy will be non-existent. Moreover, talk therapy can take a considerable amount of time before any gradual effects are noticeable. The more severe the symptoms are the more effort on the part of the patient is required to see improvement. If the symptoms are severe enough, there might not be any noticeable improvement at all.

2. Medications

Medication is another treatment option for Antisocial Personality Disorder. However, there is no specific medication for Antisocial Personality Disorder itself. Psychiatrists may choose to prescribe medications that treat the symptoms of the disorder or to treat concurrent psychological disorders that exacerbate the patient's condition. These medications are typically antipsychotics, antidepressants, or mood stabilizers. Medications such as serotonin uptake inhibitors (also known as SSRIs) can help some patients with aggressive or depressed behaviors. These inhibitors include medications such as Prozac or Zoloft, which are frequently prescribed for a range of personality disorders.

One benefit of the medication treatment is that they can have an immediate effect on the patient. Aggression, impulsivity and hostility can all be somewhat regulated by medications when properly prescribed. Another benefit is the ease of treatment. Patients do not have to put forth a great deal of effort for this treatment option to take effect – though they must at least take their medications regularly. Even if a patient is mentally unwilling to change, so long as they take their medication, some improvements may be made. This treatment option is also considerably faster than psychotherapy, which can take an extended period of time. Medication, in contrast, begins to take effect in a matter of weeks if not days of starting treatment.

The benefits of medication may prompt many to choose this treatment method. However, there are a considerable number of drawbacks to this treatment method that should be considered. Most significantly, there is no medication that has been approved by the Food and Drug Administration for the treatment of Antisocial Personality Disorder. This means that, while the medications mentioned above may have some effects on the symptoms, the disorder itself is not cured by these medications. Stopping treatment will result in a near immediate rebound of prior symptoms, and these symptoms can even be worse than before the treatment began.

Additionally, medications have serious side effects and risks that other treatment options do not possess. Zoloft, for example, has several negative possible side effects including insomnia, diarrhea, nausea, increased risk for suicide, fatigue, indigestion and more. It is also not recommended for women who are pregnant, which means a pregnant patient may be forced to stop medication while gestating, potentially undoing any prior progress. Prozac has a similar list of potential side effects. Another drawback of medications is the potential problem that arises when a patient is on medication for another condition. Medications do not always interact well with each other, and taking certain medication simultaneously can result in serious side effects. It may not be possible, for some patients to choose this treatment option if a prior health condition requires them to take a medication that would interact badly with the medication for their Antisocial Personality Disorder.

3. Behavioral Skills Lessons

A third option for the treatment of Antisocial Personality Disorder is for the patient to engage in behavioral skills lessons. These are lessons that teach individuals how to behave in a positive way in wider society and establish positive links between socially acceptable behaviors and self-benefits for the patient. This treatment option is similar to that of psychotherapy, but there are a few critical conditions that separate the two treatments.

The most critical difference between these two treatments is the provider of the treatment. While there are several options when selecting lessons in behavioral skills like behavioral schools, the patients do not have to seek treatment from a psychologist or psychiatrist. This is beneficial because the patients may be more willing to work with their instructor and may be less on guard. Especially in instances in which the patient is ordered to seek treatment by the courts, they may be reluctant to open up to a therapist. Behavioral lessons eliminate this obstacle in treatment. However, the lack of a professional can also be a drawback, as the instructor may not be fully qualified to help these individuals. Another drawback of the behavioral lessons is the limited capacity to help the patient.

While these lessons may help the patient learn to exhibit better social behaviors, they do not address underlying causes and issues of the patient. Dealing with complex issues such as the patient's anger and aggression may also be beyond the scope of behavioral classes. For these reasons, it is best if behavioral classes are parts of an overall treatment plan, rather than a sole course of treatment.

4. Support Groups

Joining a support group is also a viable treatment method for a number of Antisocial Personality

Disorder patients. Support groups offer patients a relaxed atmosphere, where they may be more open to receiving advices and making changes than in a more formal setting. Patients can find other people in these groups who better understand their disorder than those around them, and they can provide the patient with an unbiased viewpoint of their current situations. The anonymity of the group offers the patient a form of security, while the support of the group gives them motivation to continue trying to improve their situation. Moreover, these groups can also be information hubs where patients can exchange trusted information on resources available for their conditions like a good psychologist from the local area or the side effects of a particular drug. This is valuable information the patient may not receive, or may not be willing to receive, from other venues.

The risks that come with group therapy are present but indirect. Groups offer patients a platform, and while this can be both liberating and helpful, for individuals with Antisocial Personality Disorder this can also present risk. There is a possibility that individuals may join these groups to gain influence over others or a stage where they can enact their own drama. These individuals are detrimental to their treatments and to others, rather than of help. Another drawback of support groups is that the group may be unsuited to handling the more complex problems that Antisocial Personality Disorder presents. This is especially true if the patients Antisocial Personality Disorder is compounded by other disorders, such as depression or anxiety, which are both commonly found in individuals with this disorder.

5. Hospitalization

The most dramatic, and least necessary, treatment option for Antisocial Personality Disorder is hospitalization. Hospitalization of an individual with Antisocial Personality Disorder is extremely rare, and is usually only used when individuals have come into contact with the authorities. There are some instances where individuals are ordered by the court to be hospitalized for their condition before, during or after court proceedings as part of the penal process. These individuals typically display severe symptoms of their disorder, and are by no means the average patient.

That said, hospitalization offer some benefits as a treatment option. Individuals who are hospitalized can receive monitored care and can be accurately diagnosed by a professional. If other disorders exist alongside the Antisocial Personality Disorder, they are likely to be diagnosed by the hospital's psychiatrist. The patient will also receive the treatment they need- medications or extended periods of therapy. This is particularly helpful if the patient is going through an intense episode, where hospitalization allows the patient to rebalance his or herself.

There are two major shortcomings of hospitalization as a treatment option for Antisocial Personality Disorder. The first of these shortcomings lies in the short-term nature of hospitalization. It is not feasible for a patient to remain hospitalized for an extended period of time, particularly when their disorder allows them to maintain some level of functionality. Hospitalization will rarely be extended beyond a few days, which poses a significant problem for the treatment of Antisocial Personality Disorder. Treatment that only lasts for a few days, even if intensive, is unlikely to produce long-term results for the disorder. Follow-ups by the hospital or other care providers may extend the benefits received by the patients from their hospitalization, but is not a viable long-term treatment method.

Secondly, hospitalization is expensive and is not feasible for many individuals. While court order hospitalization is free or mostly so, opting to hospitalize oneself or a loved one is not. There is the possibility that the health coverage (if they are covered at all) of the individual is insufficient to pay for hospitalization and any additional fees must be paid out of pocket. Not only does this present a financial challenge to the patient, it can also place stress on the family and in the long term, may eventually exacerbate the patient's condition.

How to Choose the Right Therapy

Choosing the right therapy for an individual is a delicate task that should be taken with the utmost seriousness. Every treatment option has benefits and risks, and patients need to carefully consider which option best suits for their needs. It is also important for the patient to have a solid grasp of his or her own condition before choosing a treatment option. Antisocial Personality Disorder does not always manifest the same way in different individuals, and the unique composition of the patient's disorder should be considered when choosing a therapy method. This is especially true due to the possibility that other disorders exists for the patient as well as their Antisocial Personality Disorder, and these separate disorders can impact both the symptoms the patient displays, and the effectiveness of a treatment option.

For these reasons, the first step to selecting an appropriate therapy is to seek out professional advice.

But this first step is likely to be a difficult step for those with Antisocial Personality Disorder due to reasons like their dislike for authority figures and their difficulty in trusting others. To present themselves to a professional and trusting that professional's judgment is a difficult task for those with Antisocial Personality Disorder. However, this is a necessary step for the patient to overcome their disorder, and there is no true viable alternative. Self-diagnosis is a dangerous undertaking that runs the risk of missing other disorders as well as misdiagnosing the patient's condition. This can lead to the treatment of an incorrect disorder, which can worsen the disorder that the patient truly has.

However, it is understandable that these individuals would have some reservations on trusting another's opinion on such a serious topic. It is unreasonable to expect an individual with a disorder to trust another's opinion. Therefore, the patient should take as many steps as possible to build their confidence in their chosen professional before seeking a diagnosis. Researching the professional on the Internet, reading patient reviews, and asking about prior experiences treating patients with similar disorders are all steps a patient should take before choosing their mental health care provider.

Once a provider has been selected and a diagnosis has been made, the patient needs to seriously consider his or her treatment options. There are several elements to consider when choosing a treatment option and each of these elements will vary per individual. For instance, a patient who has an illness that requires a medication, which interacts poorly with serotonin inhibitors must consider if medication is a viable treatment option for her or him. Do his/her disorder impact their lives enough to justify taking a medication that can have potentially serious side effects? On the other hand, are they willing to put in the effort and spend the time to achieve results with other therapy options? This is a question that the patients must ask themselves when considering a therapy method for Antisocial Personality Disorder.

To answer these important questions, the patients should conduct a research. Information on treatments can be obtained via the web or at the local library for a more in-depth analysis. Patients can also ask their doctors to give them any information they may have on the advantages and disadvantages of each treatment option. Most mental health professionals will have information on treatment options available at their offices and those who don't should be capable of directing the patients to the appropriate resources. Making a list of the positive and negative aspects of each treatment option is a good tool to decide what treatment options they are most interested in pursuing and what not to take.

Another important consideration for those choosing a treatment for Antisocial Personality Disorder is the viability of the treatment according to their personalities and lifestyles, taking for instance, an extremely busy individuals without a great deal of time. Are these individuals going to involve themselves to informal treatment methods like group therapy? Will they skip meetings or ignore 'homework' so that they can focus on other tasks? If patients recognize that this is potentially the case, then what therapy method would work best for them instead of group therapy? Would they be willing and able to do more formal therapy sessions that they could schedule into their regular routine? Or are they not willing to devote so much time to the treatment of their disorder, and prefer to take medication instead? Will medication even help them manage their disorder? These are the individual concerns that each patient must consider when selecting the appropriate therapy

73

method for their disorder. Answering these questions and evaluating their individual circumstances is an important part in choosing the right therapy for an individual.

In this relevant matter, perhaps the most important element in choosing the correct therapy is for the patient to ask and carefully consider the opinion of others. It is critical to seek the opinion of a mental health professional. Just as they are capable of providing a reliable and honest evaluation, they are also the best source to identify what therapy methods would work best for the patient. A professional should be knowledgeable about the viability of each treatment method for their patients and so should be capable of giving a reliable recommendation on treatment methods. For instance, a professional should know whether the prescription of medications would benefit the patient's conditions or not. However, professionals are not the only sources who patients should seek advice from. Family and friends are also valuable resources when making these important decisions. These individuals are the closest to the patient and are usually more capable of identifying the patient's strengths and weaknesses than the patient themselves. These same individuals most often have nothing but the best intentions toward the patient, and so can be trusted to be both honest and well-motivated.

Once the patients have received their diagnosis, considered their options, researched the treatment options, considered the realistic application of the therapies, and sought the advice of those around them, they should be capable of making a decision on the appropriate treatment method for their disorder. Patients should remember that treatments are not limited to a single method and therapies that work best in conjunction with one another to maximize the results they receive from the treatment.

At this point, as critical as choosing the correct treatment option is continuing with the therapy, even when the patients do not truly wish to do so. Treatment for a disorder such as Antisocial Personality Disorder is a long process that cannot and should not be rushed. While it is only natural for patients to become impatient with their perceived lack of progress, patients need to ensure that they are allotting appropriate amount of time for therapy methods to make a difference in the patient's condition.

How to Overcome Antisocial Personality Disorder

Overcoming Antisocial Personality Disorder is a daunting task. This is not an 'illness' of the traditional sort, which once identified and treated is 'cured'. Rather, Antisocial Personality Disorder is a condition that a patient often must struggle with his or her entire life. The ability to 'cure' the disorder is limited to treating the symptoms thereof and some behavior modification. Therefore, it is perhaps misleading to say that an individual can 'overcome' their personality disorder. However, it is entirely possible for an individual to conquer the difficulties created by their disorder and learn to live a more normal lifestyle. An individual who has successfully learned to recognize his/her own problem and adapt, enabling to them to live a semi-normal life, has therefore overcome his/her Antisocial Personality Disorder. To accomplish this worthy goal, there are five steps an individual needs to take.

Admit the Problem

The first step in overcoming Antisocial Personality Disorder is to realize and admit that a problem exists in the first place. This is a difficult first step for those with Antisocial Personality Disorder, who have a hard time seeing the consequences of their negative behavior for what they are. These individuals are both narcissistic and egocentric, and these two combined traits act to create a barrier for the patient in recognizing their own culpability in negative circumstances. Even in instances for which no one should be blamed, these individuals are unlikely to take responsibility for their own negative behavior or the consequences thereof. They are more likely to shift blame to others, even when this is an irrational act. Their narcissism prevents them from seeing themselves as capable of making a mistake, while their egocentric attitude simultaneously reaffirms their right to do as they please and gives them the illusion that they are the center of everyone else's attention.

Breaking through these considerable barriers is a difficult task. Patients are often unable to do so on their own, and yet resent being forced to do so by others. This creates a paradoxical situation that is often not resolved until or unless a more formal system becomes involved. When these systems (such as Child Services or the court system) become involved, they can potentially force the patient to address their negative behavior to escape from the consequences. In these instances, the patient is capable of admitting that they have a problem and they are taking steps to address their disorder.

Seek Help from Others

The second step in overcoming Antisocial Personality Disorder is to seek help from others. A patient with Antisocial Personality Disorder is not capable of making true progress without the aid of others. The very nature of their disorder prevents them from doing so because the disorder both distorts the patient's concept of reality and reaffirms their negative behaviors. Moreover, in many instances the patient will have other disorders along with their Antisocial Personality Disorder that should also be treated and doing so without the aid of others is simply impossible.

Seeking help from others refers not only to professional help but to family, friends and group supporters as well. While a professional is necessary for the patient to overcome his/her disorder, it is ultimately those surrounding the patient on a day-to-day basis that has the greatest impact on the patient, whether that be a good thing or not. Seeking out help from others and letting them know that the patient has a disorder; a supportive can create a honest surrounding for the patient. This positive atmosphere can help foster change in the patient and helps to alert the patient and professional when the patient is struggling with treatment.

Receive a Diagnosis

Receiving an official diagnosis of Antisocial Personality Disorder is both necessary and intelligent on the part of the patient. The importance of such a diagnosis cannot be overstated. Without a diagnosis, any treatment or therapy the patient engages in is basically a blind treatment. Each and every individual has a unique set of circumstances that effects many different aspects of his/her disorder, and ignoring those circumstances to perform a self-diagnosis can result in a disaster. Moreover, there is always the potential that the patient might not have Antisocial Personality Disorder but rather a combination of other disorders.

Receiving an official diagnosis therefore works as a starting point for treatment. Until the diagnosis is made, treatment cannot begin. In fact, until the diagnosis is made, available or appropriate treatment is not even known. Seeking a professional diagnosis is one of the critical steps to overcoming Antisocial Personality Disorder. A problem cannot be truly solved, after all, until it has been properly identified.

Begin Treatment

The next critical step, in overcoming Antisocial Personality Disorder is to begin a treatment process. The available treatments and the elements a patient needs to consider when selecting a treatment plan have been covered previously. However, the importance of beginning treatment itself is something that must likewise be addressed. Many individuals with Antisocial Personality Disorder do not see their condition as detrimental to themselves or others, if they admit that they have a condition at all. It is therefore common for these patients to avoid or ignore treatment options, believing that they are fine or that they can make the necessary changes themselves.

Whether immediately apparent or not, Antisocial Personality Disorder has a serious, detrimental effect on both the patient and those around them. This disorder can cause frequent, long-lasting damage if not addressed and should not be ignored by the patient. Self-treatment is simply not realistic, and should not be considered as a viable treatment option. Changing ingrained behaviors and thought processes, not to mention potentially treating chemical imbalances, is something that an individual cannot do on their own. An outside source must be present to act as a catalyst for change and to reinforce positive changes when they occur.

Make a Concerted Effort to Change

It is absolutely true that patients with Antisocial Personality Disorder cannot change without the help of others. It is also true that the most important factors for the success of overcoming Antisocial Personality Disorder are the patients themselves. While an outside force may act as a catalyst for change and may provide both support and incentives to change, the patients must make the effort. No one can truly force another person to change if that person is unwilling to do so. Therefore, the patients must wish to alter their behaviors, and struggle to do so.

This is not an easy process. Overcoming Antisocial Personality Disorder is a drawn-out process that, by nature, includes setbacks and obstacles. A patient who wavers in his or her conviction to address his/her disorder and make positive changes can and will backslide in his/her progress. Patients should be prepared to make serious, dramatic, and difficult changes to their own behaviors and thought processes in an effort to overcome their disorder. Only then can they succeed in establishing a positive lifestyle that promotes both their welfare and of others.

How to Find Your Escape

To escape from Antisocial Personality Disorder, a person must first understand what they are escaping from. In the case of Antisocial Personality Disorder, patients need to escape from their self-created realities. In this internal world, the patient sees herself or himself as the central figure, and this colors his or her actions and perceptions in the real world. For example, if the patient thinks of himself as a victim in his own internal world, he will act as the victim in the real world, regardless of whether he has been victimized or not. If the patient sees himself as the only important person in their internal world, he is unlikely to care much about others in the external world. The discrepancies between these worlds naturally create obstacles for the patients to overcome and challenges for those around them in the real world.

To escape from this internal world, patients have variety of options. For example, patients may choose to escape their internal world by consciously choosing to exercise their skills in empathy. As previously discussed, those with Antisocial Personality Disorder often lack empathy. The patients are unlikely to unconsciously empathize with another individual. However, by intentionally expanding their viewpoints and consciously making an effort to develop their empathy, the patients may increase their natural empathic levels while also escaping from their own worlds.

This, of course, is easier said than done. Utilizing an emotional tool that they are not proficient in is a difficult task and feeling an emotional impact may be beyond their abilities when they begin this exercise. In this instance, the patients should try to make it an intellectual exercise to place themselves in the minds of others, and to grasp the thought processes and emotional states of others. Doing so, even while purely an intellectual pursuit; open the patients up to the world of others, allowing them to escape from the false illusion that they are the center figure in all realities. Eventually, this may allow the patients to engage their emotions, granting them an even greater escape from their own minds and concerns into the psyche of another person.

If the patient is unwilling or unable to engage in actively extending his/her empathy towards another person, other viable alternatives exist. For example, instead of focusing his/her empathy on a physical person, the patient may choose to use literature or other media to practice his/her empathy. Books are important tools as they allow the patient to gain a more in-depth understanding of another person (even if they are only fictional characters) and see situations through the viewpoint of someone else. Patients who do not enjoy reading may choose to listen to audio books or can focus on watching more emotionally stimulating movies or television shows. Simply watching live action plays are also good methods for the patient to escape from their own world while learning an important socialization skill.

Another way to escape from this internal world is to utilize meditation. Meditation is focused on re-centering oneself and expelling negative thoughts and emotions. When a person achieves a truly meditative state, his/her mind is 'blank' through funneling out his/her negative emotions. This does two very important things for the patients of Antisocial Personality Disorder. First, this allows the patient to rest from his/her internal dialogue that is most typically dominated by his/her own concerns. This internal dialogue is unhealthy, and is usually a direct contributor to negative behavior. Eliminating this negative influence for even short periods of time can be a positive thing for the patient.

Secondly, meditation grants the patient the ability to calm their nerves and think about the decisions thoroughly before they are made. For those with Antisocial Personality Disorder, rash, reckless and impulsive behavior is often the cause of many of their problems. Being able to stop and think before making a decision and using the tools taught to them through meditation, allows the patient to make calmer, more rational decisions. These decisions are less likely to have the negative results and can help the patients avoid serious complications in their lives.

Developing healthy, productive hobbies is also an acceptable method of escape for those with Antisocial Personality Disorder. The hobby that the patients choose should be an activity that is both engaging and positive, and should offer the patient the opportunity to focus entirely on subjects other than themselves. Knitting, sewing, mechanics, building and others are all viable options for patients to choose as an acceptable method of escaping from their disorder.

This is particularly true if the patient can use this hobby to engage with others in a positive manner. For example, a patient who chooses knitting as her (or his) hobby may be able to utilize this skill for charitable purposes. Knitting clothes for underprivileged children, for example offers double the benefit for the patient. The first benefit they receive from this hobby is the opportunity to focus on a task outside of their own internal world, escaping from their worries, doubts, and egocentric attitude.

The second benefit is received when the patient donates his/her effort to those in need. Receiving the gratitude, thanks and emotional connection to the person they helped can be a positive influence on the patient. It can also help the patient establish an emotional link to another person, which can be a decisive element in treatment. If a genuine emotional connection is made with someone else, the patient will typically value that connection due to its rarity. Feeling needed, capable and important to the individual who they have helped can help establish an emotional bond to that person, resulting in many positive influences on the patient. In short, by utilizing their hobbies to perform charitable acts, patients may be able to establish an emotional connection with others, thereby escaping from their own internal worlds and overcoming, or at least reducing the effects of their disorder.

Conclusion

Antisocial Personality Disorder is a serious mental health condition that has a profound, life-long effect on the patients. Individuals with Antisocial Personality Disorder are characterized by a repeated pattern of behavior that is hostile to society. These individuals are typically highly egocentric with correspondingly high levels of narcissism and detachment. Antisocial Personality Disorder patients are often rash and impulsive, frequently making bad decisions that have negative consequences in the long-term. For example, patients may make the decision to engage in illegal or illicit activities, which provide them with immediate satisfaction. The patient does not think of the long-term consequences of their actions, which can include jail time, job loss and more.

Patients with Antisocial Personality Disorder are also known to be manipulative, using any means necessary to achieve their goals. For this reason, despite their frequently hostile, aggressive and irritable behavior, patients may display a great deal of charm in an effort to manipulate those around them. This manipulation can often have a distinct purpose, such as increasing the patients' funds and resources, or can be done simply because the patients know that they can. For those with Antisocial Personality Disorder, manipulating others is a method to reaffirm their superiority and is done on the part of the patient with no remorse.

Antisocial Personality Disorder can affect the ability of individuals to engage in society, making their success in life a daunting task. This is not only the case in terms of monetary or societal success, but also in the case of forming healthy emotional attachments. As a result of this disorder, every relationship that the patients have, from their parents, to their significant others, to their children, is impacted in a negative way. For example, it is common for patients with Antisocial

Personality Disorder to be abusive or neglectful in parental endeavors. These individuals simply do not make good parents, as they naturally place their wants and concerns above that of the children.

Likewise, these individuals are also likely to have extremely dysfunctional romantic relationships. Being naturally manipulative, while also having the ability to retain an emotional distance from others, means that in relationships these individuals can be both cold and dominating personalities. They can and will use blatant manipulation on their partners to gain the results they hope for, regardless of whether that manipulation is sexual or emotional in nature. They are also frequently unfaithful as they have a hard time truly developing an emotional attachment to their partners and so are more likely to abandon those partners in pursuit of more exciting or beneficial relationships.

In addition, antisocial patients are likely to have difficulty with authority figures. This issue often begins with the parents in early childhood, and then later continues with other authority figures. This issue with authority figures can often result in dropping out from formal education, as they are likely to take issue with educators who have a degree of power over them. There is also a pattern of reoccurring problems with law enforcement. These individuals carry a great deal of resentment toward those who have established a position that is in any way superior to them, and these include those who enforce the rules of society. This disregard for authority may lead the patient to take petty rebellious actions. In childhood, this rebellion may come in the form of stealing, lying, or manipulating their parents. In adulthood, this need manifests in behaviors such as shoplifting, in an effort to reinforce their abilities to 'get one over' on those in charge.

These patients may also display overly aggressive behaviors, resulting in physical violence. Individuals with Antisocial Personality Disorder are often physically aggressive and may be abusive in relationships. This abusive tendency may take the form of verbal abuse and it is often physical in nature. This physical violence often leads these individuals to the attention of law enforcement. Often times, those with Antisocial Personality Disorder will have repeated engagements with law enforcement officers and the courts, and these repeat engagements are likely to be the eventual reason for their diagnosis.

All the same, Antisocial Personality Disorder will not manifest the same way in all individuals. For this reason, there are five subtypes of Antisocial Personality Disorder that are used to gain a greater understanding of an individual patient. The five subtypes of Antisocial Personality Disorder, identified by psychologist Theodore Millon are the malevolent antisocial, the covetous antisocial, the risk-taking antisocial, the reputation-defending antisocial, and the nomadic antisocial. Each of the subtypes of this disorder has its unique challenges, and cannot be treated or addressed in the same manner as the other subtypes.

Those who are malevolent antisocial individuals are both aggressive and dominating. They display sadistic tendencies and typically enjoy harming and manipulating others. The malevolent subtype of Antisocial Personality Disorder, are the typical over-aggressive individuals, who have problems with controlling their impulses when upset or angry. Those of the covetous subtype are begrudging and envious of others. These patients believe that they are held back by others, and have a slightly victimized attitude, which they use to justify their behaviors. The covetous subtype is the 'purest' form of Antisocial Personality Disorder, and generally lacks input from other personality types such as the sadistic features of the malevolent subtype. The risk-taking subtype dominant trait is taking ill-thought out, dangerous actions that can have dire consequences for the patients. This subtype has histrionic features and they are likely to make quick, foolhardy decisions. Accidents and mistakes are common occurrences for those in the risk-taking subtype of Antisocial Personality Disorder.

The reputation-defending subtype feels a great need to be seen as impervious. They care deeply about how others perceive them, and they become very combative when their reputation is imperiled. Their narcissistic features that force them to maintain a façade of invincibility dominate the reputation-defending subtype. While the reputation-defending subtype patients have very narcissistic nature, there may be an underlying lack of self-confidence that encourages the insecurities of these individuals.

The nomadic subtype of Antisocial Personality Disorder has both schizoid and avoidant features. They are often found to be vagrants and vagabonds and are drifters who stay on the edge of society. Those in this subtype often frequently change jobs and locations, and feel no attachment for a specific area or position. For this reason, they are often homeless and poor, with little to no formal education and have limited connections to other people. Their drifting tendencies may even take them away from their families, the group of people most likely to help the patient adjust and achieve some level of normalcy. The result is a worsening of their conditions, and this can often lead to an early death and more frequent encounters with law enforcement than is typical of even other antisocial patients.

The cause of Antisocial Personality Disorder has not been officially discovered. However, it is likely that there are a variety of factors, including both genetic and environmental causes that result in an individual developing Antisocial Personality Disorder. Theories to explain the development of Antisocial Personality

Disorder include heredity, minor forms of brain damage, serotonin inhibitor issues, and prenatal smoking. Environmental theories to explain Antisocial Personality Disorder focus on the early development of the child with emphasis placed on the lack of trust, security, and an emotional bond with the parents in particular. There has not been a formal recognition of which of these theories, are believed to be a definitive cause of Antisocial Personality Disorder. What is clear is that this disorder is not something that can be 'cured' in the traditional sense and instead must be managed throughout the patients' lives. In an effort to manage this disorder, several treatment options exist.

The treatments available to help patients manage their Antisocial Personality Disorder include psychotherapy, also known as talk therapy, medications, hospitalization, group therapy and behavioral lessons. These treatments have both advantages and disadvantages that patients should consider before engaging in. Due to the limited scope of each individual treatment option, patients may wish to engage in a more comprehensive plan that includes multiple forms of treatment simultaneously. However, even when patients apply themselves to multiple treatment methods, immediate results are unlikely to appear. Treatment of Antisocial Personality Disorder is notoriously difficult and requires serious effort and conviction on the part of the patient to see improvement.

Antisocial Personality Disorder is a serious condition that presents a solemn challenge to both the patient and to those around them. Left unchecked, Antisocial Personality Disorder can dominate the lives of both the patient and their loved ones. However, if patients recognize their disorders and make a genuine effort to change, while being supported by those in their immediate surroundings, a great deal of improvement can still be made. While the disorder itself is unlikely to disappear, the patients can learn to control their symptoms in a positive manner. Controlling the symptoms of Antisocial Personality Disorder can provide a measure of peace to the patients' families (who are often affected as greatly as the patient) and contribute to the integration of the affected patient into society.

Final Word/About the Author

I was born and raised in Norwalk, Connecticut. Growing up, I could often be found spending afternoons reading in the local public library about management techniques and leadership styles, along with overall outlooks towards life. It was from spending those afternoons reading about how others have led productive lives that I was inspired to start studying patterns of human behavior and self-improvement. Usually I write works around sports to learn more about influential athletes in the hopes that from my writing, you the reader can walk away inspired to put in an equal if not greater amount of hard work and perseverance to pursue your goals. However, I began writing about psychology topics such as Antisocial Personality Disorder so that I could help others better understand why they act and think the way they do and how to build on their strengths while also identifying their weaknesses. If you enjoyed

Antisocial Personality Disorder: The Ultimate Guide to Symptoms, Treatment and Prevention please leave a review! Also, you can read more of my general works on *Best Places to Retire: The Top 15 Affordable Towns for Retirement in Asia, Best Places to Retire: The Top 15 Affordable Towns for Retirement in Europe, Best Places to Retire: The Top 15 Affordable Towns for Retirement in Florida, Best Places to Retire: The Top 15 Affordable Towns for Retirement on a Budget, Gratitude, How to Fundraise, How to Get Out of the Friend Zone, Histrionic Personality Disorder, Narcissistic Personality Disorder, Avoidant Personality Disorder, Sundown Syndrome, ISTJs, ISFJs, ISFPs, INTJs, INFPs, INFJs, ESFPs, ESFJs, ESTJs, ENFPs, ENFJs, ENTJs, How to be Witty, How to be Likeable, How to be Creative, Bargain Shopping, Productivity Hacks, Morning Meditation, Becoming a Father,* and *33 Life Lessons: Success Principles,*

Career Advice & Habits of Successful People in the Kindle Store.

Like what you read?

I write because I love researching and sharing psychology topics to better understand why we act the way we do. My readers inspire me to write more so please do not hesitate to let me know what you thought by leaving a review! If you love books on life, basketball, or productivity, check out my website at claytongeoffreys.com to join my exclusive list where I let you know about my latest books. Aside from being the first to hear about my latest releases, you can also download a free copy of *33 Life Lessons: Success Principles, Career Advice & Habits of Successful People*. See you there!

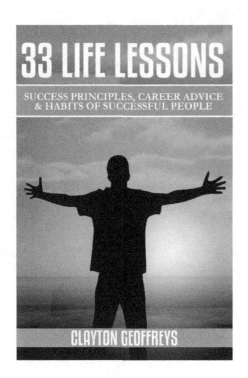

Made in the USA
Monee, IL
25 October 2023

45215437R00063